THE WOLF YOU FEED

Darcy Parker Bruce

BROADWAY PLAY PUBLISHING INC
New York
www.broadwayplaypublishing.com
info@broadwayplaypublishing.com

THE WOLF YOU FEED
© Copyright 2024 Darcy Parker Bruce

First edition: August 2024
I S B N: 979-8-88856-025-9

Book design: Marie Donovan
Page make-up: Adobe InDesign
Typeface: Palatino

THE WOLF YOU FEED had a staged reading on 1 March 2020 by Theater Prometheus (Artistic Director, Tracey Erbacher) in co-production with The Actor's Center in Washington, DC. The cast and creative contributors were:

PAMPLEMOUSSE .... Pauline Lamb
BRYAN/AJAX ....Daniel Prillaman
ARTHUR/CRACKER JACK .... Jane E Petkofsky
BENJI/RIFF RAF...Jordan Brown
LISA/JET .... Emily Dalton
MAX ....Becca Ballinger

Director .... Patrick Gallagher Landes
Stage Manager ....Katie Gallagher
Sound Designer ....Jordana Abrenica
Costume Designer.. Leila Spolter
Set Designer.. Eric McMorris
Lighting Designer...Yannick Godts
Dramaturg .... Mariele Fluegeman
Actor's Center Rep.. Zoe Walpole

A planned full production was cancelled due to Covid.

CHARACTERS & SETTING

Max, *any/30s, recently separated. Currently living in the run-down Shady Pines motel.*

Lisa, *any/ 30s, Max's associate from work. She's very buttoned up. Doesn't understand why Max is hiding out at Shady Pines. Trying to get Max to return to work. Brings her casseroles etc.*

Arthur, *any/50s, door-to-door salesman. Carries a briefcase. What's in the briefcase? They would really like to show Max. She does not care to know. Arthur is charming but creepy. Calm down Arthur.*

Benji, *any/20s, hippie/ vegan/ tarot card reader. Is totes "off the grid".*

Bryan, *any/30s. Max's ex.*

Pamplemousse, *any/?, a wolf. Has trouble with eye contact. Named after a can of La Croix.*

Cracker Jack, *any/?, pack member. Eye patch.*

Ajax, *any/?, pack member. Angry. Maybe yells a lot.*

Riffraf, *any/?, pack member. Maybe they play the drums.*

Jet, *any/?, pack member. Plays the guitar. Has a headband.*

The Wolf Pack, *their official pack name is 1736b. They're one of 11 packs that runs in the park. They are human shapes in wolf masks. They've taught themselves to read by going through garbage and they've assigned themselves names inspired by the garbage they've gone through. They have unique identifiers ie.* JET *has a headband etc. They're very punk rock. Think leather jackets and patches and doc martins and bad 'tudes dudes. Wolves playing instruments are CONSTANTLY filling space with SOUND. Until they aren't.*

Notes on doubling:
The following roles can be doubled:
ARTHUR *and* CRACKER JACK
BENJI *and* RIFFRAF
LISA *and* JET
BRYAN *and* AJAX

The Shady Pines motel at the edge of a national park somewhere foggy with lots of pines.

The forest can be suggested by shadow or projection, especially when it begins to take over MAX's *motel room.*

Time: Now.

PLAYWRIGHT'S NOTE

All the actors in this piece should be played by dancers, and all of the dancers in this piece should identify as non-binary, trans, genderqueer etc. This is a work inclusive of all bodies, shapes, and sizes, and should not be thought of as a dance piece accessible only to able-bodied dancers. Additionally, I've left character's genders open, and although they're gendered in the script, please adjust accordingly as needed.

The wolf masks and Max's fur coat should be very untraditional. Think metal suggestions of the outline of a wolf's snout, or a bright pink faux fur cropped jacket for Max. HAVE FUN. Everyone probably has leg warmers.

Whenever wolves are running it shouldn't look like running but more of a complication of twists and turn and body angles and leaps and almost dancing but savage.

When the wolves move through a playing space they do so like a rowdy gang. Someone can't stop hitting every surface with their drumsticks to see what it will sound like, someone else is trying to get attention by rough housing, maybe someone else is compulsively howling, like hiccups. Whatever movements you find unique to your wolf pack should be allowed to fill the space when the wolves take over, and it should always be messy.

[…] denotes a pause, often a moment charged with energy. Can be a silence, or an action moment depending on the character. I've been using […] more than beats recently, because I like the way it allows an actor to fill the silence.

Dialogue with a dash at the end represents rapid interruption. A slash within a line indicates overlapping speech. Lack of punctuation is intentional, and an indicator that the words be read in a rush, or as a run on sentence. Lack of capital letters may indicate a character isn't feeling very confident.

Words in (parentheses) are not spoken vocally but still made known.

At first when the wolf pack howls it sounds like humans mimicking the howling of wolves but gradually grows more and more realistic.

"And the walls became the world all around."
Maurice Sendak, *Where the Wild Things Are*

scene i

*(A room in the Shady Pines motel. Early afternoon. Very
run down and shabby. Behind it the forest looms large. In
the distance, the howling of a pack of wolves
Early spring. The last of the winter is melting and the sun is
coaxing the earth back to life.
In the makeshift shambly kitchen of room 8 LISA is making
MAX a cup of shitty coffee. MAX sits at the tiny kitchen
table. On the table is a pan covered with aluminum foil. It's
a casserole.)*

LISA: You're growing wild Maxine.

MAX: I don't mind it.

LISA: This room is so dark.

MAX: The darkness helps my headaches.

LISA: *(Of the casserole)* You should put that in the fridge.

MAX: It won't fit.

LISA: It's going to go bad

MAX: I'm not going to eat it.

LISA: It's tuna fish

(MAX says nothing.)

LISA: With potato chips on top.

(MAX says nothing.)

LISA: You used to love that.

MAX: I'll take it black.

LISA: What?
Oh.
Sure.
(*She sits down with two cups of coffee. Takes a sip of hers and makes a face.*)
This coffee is awful.
.

Just come home

MAX: I am home.
I live here now

LISA: No.
You're being so dramatic.
Just
Listen. I'm sure Bryan won't be mad. He understands why you left /he'll let you come back—

MAX: /I'm not going back there.

LISA: Maxine.

MAX: I'm not going back there.

LISA: Okay then you can stay with me until you two make up /we can keep working on our proposal—

MAX: /We're not going to make up. And I think I've changed my mind—

LISA: —about what?

(*No answer*)

LISA: What do you mean you think you've changed your mind?

MAX: I think I was wrong.
About—

LISA: —about?
You're talking nonsense.
You're throwing your whole life away.

MAX: Maybe.

LISA: It's like I don't even know who you are anymore.

MAX: Me neither.

LISA: You're almost out of PTO.

.

I'm doing the lion's share of the work.

MAX: I'm not going back.

LISA: You're being ridiculous! How will you survive?
Even if you stay here. You can't afford to—

MAX: —Lisa.

LISA: if you're really done with him then just sign the
papers—

MAX: —I will—

LISA: —and you can come and stay with me.
It doesn't matter what you decide. Okay? I'm sorry I
got annoyed with you. I support you. You can sleep on
our couch. We'll keep working. Craig won't mind. Sign
the papers and just come home. We are a team. Okay?
Come back home and finish what we started.

MAX: Oh.
Lisa.
Hear that?

LISA: Hear what?

MAX: That howling?

LISA: Wolves? This close to the edge of the forest?

MAX: They're everywhere.

.

I just need more time. Okay?

LISA: Sure.

(LISA *and* MAX *sit in silence and drink their coffee.*
The sounds of the forest waking from a long winter grow
louder and louder.)

LISA: UGH
It's so LOUD.

MAX: *(With delight)* It really is.

LISA: Sign. Don't sign.
come back
Stay here.
I don't know.
Fine Max.
What do you want me to say
/I'm your best friend

MAX: /you don't have to say anything.
.

LISA: Aren't I your best friend?

MAX: .
of course.

LISA: Max!

MAX: Best best friends.

LISA: This place is changing you.
Who names a motel Shady Pines.
This place is a dump.
The sooner we bulldoze it the better off everyone will
be.

MAX: Lisa.
I don't think we should move forward.
With Aspen Grove.
It's just.
After what happened with Bryan—
I feel safe here.
It may be a rundown flea ridden motel in the middle of
nowhere
But
It doesn't cost much of anything.
And I can't be the only person running away from—

The only person who needs somewhere.
Somewhere safe. You know?

LISA: .
Well that is just ridiculous.

.

.

Do you remember Benji?

MAX: Your oracle?

LISA: That's right.
Benji
Well. He's totally off the grid now.
He set up camp around here.
And
I hope you won't be too mad about this but. I made
you an appointment. Okay?
So.

MAX: How?

LISA: Hm?

MAX: How did you make an appointment with Benji,
your oracle, if he is totally off the grid?

LISA: Through his assistant.

.

anyway. Our appointment is in an hour. We should go.

MAX: Where?

LISA: I have the GPS coordinates on my phone.
There's an app for this.

MAX: There's an app for finding your off the grid
oracle in the woods?

LISA: We just have to watch out for the wolves.
But wolves hate people right?
They're shy?
They won't bother us.
I have this air horn. And this mace

MAX: They're wolves Lisa.
Not rapists.

LISA: Still.
(Of the casserole) you should put that in the fridge.

MAX: It won't—
Okay.

*(LISA punches the coordinates in her phone and it makes a
beeping sound. LISA puts on her jacket and exits.
MAX regards the casserole.
She pulls back the foil and examines it.
She makes a face of disgust.
She takes the casserole and slips it under her coat.
When she leaves the motel room, she places it next to the
door so LISA won't see.
A car horn
MAX exits.
A few moments. The WOLF PACK trickles in.
They examine the casserole.
They begin to eat it.
The sound of drumming like wolves running after deer like a
heart beating fast like the wind like the rain like the forest.
Darkness)*

scene ii

*(The middle of the woods
MAX and LISA stand together but apart. Two people who
used to be friends but don't really know how to keep doing it.
LISA is out of her element. MAX looks at home in the woods.)*

LISA: HELLO?
BENJI?
Oh god I hope he didn't move somewhere else since
they updated the app
I don't like it out here
I think I can feel something watching us

MAX: It's just the forest

LISA: Jesus listen to you it's just the forest
You're not living in a fantasy novel
BENJI?
We need to find him. So he can talk some sense into
you
So you can brush your hair and put on clean clothes
and come home.

MAX: There *is* someone watching us—
—in the woods and all around them the wolf pack
gathers.

LISA: BENJI!
Oh god please be here I just need to like
Re-center
I need to reground myself because I am losing my shit
BENJI!

(The WOLF PACK *begins to circle.*
LISA *cannot see them.*
MAX *can.)*

MAX: There's magic here. I can feel it.

*(*MAX *watches the* WOLF PACK. LISA *is absorbed in her
phone.
The light from* LISA*'s phone is glaringly artificial against the
rest of the forest.
The* WOLF PACK *regards* MAX. PAMPLEMOUSSE
*approaches.
The rest of the* WOLF PACK *watches.)*

MAX: Is it you?

*(*PAMPLEMOUSSE *and* MAX *regard one another.
But there is a rustling.
The* WOLF PACK *backs away.)*

LISA: BENJI!

(BENJI *crashes into clearing.*
The WOLF PACK *fades into the forest.*
MAX *watches them go.)*

BENJI: Lisa! Greetings!

(BENJI *enters.)*

LISA: BENJI thank god.

BENJI: This must be Max.

MAX: How (*do you know who I am*)
???

BENJI: My third eye is totally open.
Let's see
(*He puts his fingers to his temples.)*
Maxine Walker
thirty-four
recently single
mmm. mhhm. Mhmm. Okay okay okay yeah.

MAX: Yeah?

BENJI: Yeesh!

MAX: Yeesh?

BENJI: I don't know that is some weird karmic energy.
You smell weird
You smell like.
Dirt. Blood. Sweat.
.

mmmmm
you smell like fear.
You're running from something.

MAX: Someone.

BENJI: The wolf at the door.

MAX: He's no wolf.
Wolves are kinder.

BENJI: yep I sense bad vibes.
Definite bad vibes.
(*Perhaps too gleefully*)
Ooh
And violence.

MAX: /Violence?

LISA: /See. Max. This is why you need to get out of
here.
Leave your shitty little run down motel.
Come back to civilization.

MAX: (*To* BENJI) What kind of violence?

(BENJI *is taking* MAX *in.*)

LISA: .
Okay I have a meeting.
Max. Look at me.
Look at me.
Max.
We. We have a meeting. I need you.
Will you come?

(MAX *says nothing.*)

LISA: (*Exasperated*) fine.
You love this place so much just stay here.
But it's coming down. That shitty motel and all the
land surrounding it.

MAX: Lisa!

LISA: (*To* MAX) We'll update your office. I'll buy you
one of those, those little machines that makes outdoor
noises. Y'know, birds and waterfalls and I don't know
thunderstorms. I'll hire someone to paint branches on
the walls Max, I support you and your little obsession
with running away. You'll see. it'll be the same but
you'll have running water. I'll buy you a Keurig—

BENJI: —I fucking hate Keurigs—

LISA: —whatever you need, what else do you want do you want a hamster—

MAX: —Lisa. You've got to stop them.
Aspen can't happen—

LISA: —stop them?
Max. This project was YOUR idea.
Benji. Help her please. Unblock her chakras or whatever it is that she needs. Fuck. Benji. Fix her. UGH this forest is driving me insane. There are bugs in my eyes and my heels are ruined!
(Trying to center herself)
Okay. Okay. Max. Just. I'm sorry—again—I know you're on a
(Searching)
journey. Right now. And I can't rush you. But Aspen Grove is OUR project. I can't let you throw it away.
(Hostile)
So get your shit together and come back down to Earth because I am sick of doing all of this work by myself.
(Beat) I have to go talk to a room full of men about condos. I'll see you tomorrow.
.
(Gnats in her eyes)
BUGS!
(Exits with much contempt)

BENJI: (Offering a bag to MAX) Date roll?

MAX: I'm not hungry.

BENJI: I don't think that's true.

MAX: What—

BENJI: (He grabs her wrist, lapses into a trance)
You are hungry.
You're so hungry
Blood and teeth and strength and bones twisting on themselves and the rush of the wind at night and the

feel of the ground under your feet as you run with
the pack your family everyone you've ever known
everything you've ever known leading to this the
moment the momentum building you're hungry so
hungry for the blood of the kill it's blood for blood
and if you don't kill him he's going to kill you cut you
open—

MAX: *(She twists away, shaken)* —DON'T TOUCH ME.

(When MAX *yells the forest shifts.*
Silence
MAX *and* BENJI *stare at one another.)*

BENJI: You're leaving them aren't you?

MAX: What are you talking about?

BENJI: The human world? It's not for you, is it?

MAX: I…

*(*BENJI *shakes off the trance.)*

BENJI: Date roll?

*(*MAX *just stares.*
Behind them the WOLF PACK *gathers.*
MAX *turns to face the* WOLF PACK.*)*

MAX: What do you want from me?

(A guitar chord
Darkness)

scene iii:
a pack of wolves

(Back in the motel. Evening. The moon hangs low and
luminous.
MAX *is going through a stack of paperwork. She's got a pen.*
She puts it to paper. She pauses.
Her stomach growls.

She drops the pen. Goes in search of something to eat
She finds:
Leftover casserole.
Some kind of protein bar
Packets of sugar and creamer for the coffee
A handful of mints
Coffee grounds.
She eats all of it.
But none of it is good enough.
She's still hungry.
She searches for more.
She goes through the trash.
She eats some more trash.
Her stomach growls.
A knock on the door
MAX answers.
There's no one there.)

MAX: Hello?
Lisa?
Benji?
.
Bryan?

(Someone starts drumming something with their drumsticks.)

MAX: Hello?

(The entire WOLF PACK comes forward out of the shadows. They watch her. CRACKER JACK steps forward. He has an eye-patch.)

CRACKER JACK: Hey

MAX: Hey

CRACKER JACK: We're a pack of wolves

MAX: I can see that.

CRACKER JACK: Do you want to be a king?

MAX: Uh.

CRACKER JACK: We saw you today.

MAX: I remember.

CRACKER JACK: We like the way you smell.
We like that you are very quiet.
.

It's a full moon.
…
so
what do you say?
Do you want to come out and run with us?

MAX: I don't know if that's such a good idea.

CRACKER JACK: We thought you might say that.
We brought you some gifts.
(He clears his throat.
PAMPLEMOUSSE *comes forward.*
She has a paper bag. She removes the items.)

CRACKER JACK: apple core
left sock
teddy bear
bag of pills.
.

So.
What do you think?

MAX: Oh.
These are.
Nice
Gifts.
Thank you.

CRACKER JACK: Be careful with the bag of pills.
Riffraf tried one and fell asleep for two days.
We thought she was dead.

MAX: I'll be careful.

CRACKER JACK: So.
The moon's pretty cool. right?

MAX: I like to run. But I won't howl.

(*A pause while the* WOLF PACK *considers this.*
Maybe they whisper amongst themselves.)

PAMPLEMOUSSE: Not yet.

MAX: Not ever.
I'm no wolf.

PAMPLEMOUSSE: You're no human either.

MAX: What do you mean?

PAMPLEMOUSSE: You used to be.
But things are changing.
.
I can smell it on you.

(*Some wolf starts a howl. It's probably* JET.
She doesn't have any patience.
All the other wolves are compelled to join in.
MAX *watches. She slips on her running shoes.*
The howling stops.)

MAX: Just for a little while.

PAMPLEMOUSSE: Just for a little while.

(*The* WOLF PACK *takes off.*
PAMPLEMOUSSE *waits for* MAX.)

MAX: A King?

PAMPLEMOUSSE: (*Smiles*) King. Be king. With me and
with riffraff and with cracker jack

MAX: I don't understand

PAMPLEMOUSSE: Run with us. Under the moon. And we
will all be king.

MAX: Who are you?

PAMPLEMOUSSE: We're called pack number 1736b.
we're one of eleven packs in this park. But we're the
best. We're the smartest. We taught ourselves how to
read. Do you want to know how?

MAX: Yes.

PAMPLEMOUSSE: Garbage. We taught ourselves. We're
the closest to the forest edge. So we have the best
access to garbage. My name is Pamplemousse.

MAX: My name is MAX

(MAX *holds her hand out to shake but* PAMPLEMOUSSE
doesn't know what to do with it.)

MAX: Oh. Sorry. I don't know how to officially greet a
wolf.

PAMPLEMOUSSE: Don't make eye contact.
Lower your head
Lie on your back.

(MAX *does these things. She is on the ground, belly up.)*

PAMPLEMOUSSE: Good.
Now I do this.
(She puts her jaws around MAX's *neck.*
She does not bite down.
A few moments pass.
Then she backs away)
Okay.
That's it.

MAX: Can I move now?

PAMPLEMOUSSE: Yes.

MAX: *(She sits up and brushes leaves off her body)*
How did you get the name Pamplemousse?

PAMPLEMOUSSE: I gave it to myself.
I saw it on a can.
Something called

(Pronounced phonetically)
LA CRO-IX

MAX: *La Croix.*
Okay.
It's a good name.

PAMPLEMOUSSE: Yes.

MAX: What are the others called?

PAMPLEMOUSSE: With the eye patch? That's Cracker
Jack.

MAX: Is he the alpha?

PAMPLEMOUSSE: What? No.
He's really big on social media.

MAX: Oh. cool.

PAMPLEMOUSSE: Then there's Ajax.
And Jet.
And Riffraf.
.
Jet plays the guitar.

MAX: Okay.

PAMPLEMOUSSE: Are you afraid?

MAX: *(She considers)* No. I thought I might be. But I'm
not.

PAMPLEMOUSSE: Well, you smell like fear.

MAX: That's from earlier.

PAMPLEMOUSSE: What happened?

MAX: Running. But different from what you do.
.
and
Every time I think about…
Going back to work. Or going back to…
What used to be home, to, to get my things…
Or…

Going back, at all….
I don't know.
I don't know if I can do it.
.

and I'm sick of tuna casserole.

PAMPLEMOUSSE: .
that makes sense.
All of those things sound horrible.
You should stay here
In the forest.
Stay here with me.
With us.
With the pack. Join our pack.
Join our band.

MAX: I don't really know you.

PAMPLEMOUSSE: Okay. We'll keep asking.
But we can't wait forever.
We move with the deer.
.

When you're ready to join
just howl when we howl.
Okay?

MAX: Why do you think I'll join you?

PAMPLEMOUSSE: The forest said.
So.
When you're ready to join
just howl when we howl.
Okay?

MAX: What did it say?

PAMPLEMOUSSE: (Pause) It said you were tired and
angry and looking for change.
Is that true?

MAX: .
Yes.

PAMPLEMOUSSE: So. When you're ready to join, just howl when we howl.

MAX: I'll howl.
When I'm ready.

PAMPLEMOUSSE: This is a contract between us now.
Don't be surprised I know about contracts.
I read newspapers.
People throw those away.

MAX: Is it hard to learn from garbage?

PAMPLEMOUSSE: It's the only way I know.

MAX: I imagine there are a lot of things I still don't know how to do.

PAMPLEMOUSSE: Yep.

(PAMPLEMOUSSE *throws back her head and howls*
the pack joins in. This goes on for a moment.
Then.)

PAMPLEMOUSSE: Okay.
When you're ready.
Oh. And Jet says if you get more casserole we'll eat it.
We like garbage.
It really tasted like garbage but we'll eat it okay?

MAX: Okay.
.
Why?

PAMPLEMOUSSE: Why?

MAX: Why me?
Why do you want me to be a part of your pack?

PAMPLEMOUSSE: You fed us.
And now we'll feed you.
Pack takes care of pack.

MAX: I'm so hungry.
I didn't think I was.

But I AM.

I'm so hungry but. Not for casserole.

PAMPLEMOUSSE: *(Knowingly)* No.

MAX: No.

.

PAMPLEMOUSSE: Let's run now.

MAX: *(Nods)* Okay.
(She looks at the stars.)
Let's run forever. And never stop.

PAMPLEMOUSSE: You're gonna make a great wolf.

(Darkness)

scene iv:
owls and fur coats

(MAX returns from her run with the pack. It's late.
She's sweaty and out of breath. But happy.
She has to pass the kitchen table.
Her phone buzzes.
She freezes.
She is still until the phone stops buzzing.
She moves again. Through the bedroom and towards the
bathroom.
She doesn't realize that there is an oak tree where the toilet
used to be.
The oak's branches hang low over the bathroom. She has to
weave in and out of them.
She moves in and out of the motel room brushing her teeth.
Changing into her pajamas.
She goes back into the bathroom.
Beat.
A long low mournful hoot.
She backtracks out of the bathroom. Bumps into a branch.
She notices the oak tree.

No longer a toothbrush, she's holding a handful of chives.
She stares at them. Lets them fall.
Wipes her mouth. Stares into the bathroom.
The owl hoots again.
A buzzing as MAX's *phone rings once more. She freezes.*
Ignores it. It stops. A moment passes. It buzzes again. This
repeats. She moves further and further from the phone. She
tries to hide. Another mournful hoot from the bathroom.
MAX *puts a pillow over her head.*
The phone buzzes and buzzes and buzzes.
MAX *throws the pillow.*
She goes over to her phone and screams.
Her scream becomes a strangled howl and the forest joins in.
Her phone is silent.
A knock on the door. MAX *just stares at it.*
Maybe it's the WOLF PACK.
Slowly, MAX *answers.*
ARTHUR *is standing at the door. He is relentlessly perky.*
Big smiles. Standing straight. Holding a briefcase. He's
very buttoned up. And CONFIDENT. ARTHUR *is*
CONFIDENT.)

MAX: Hello?

ARTHUR: Greetings! Arthur, miss and at your service.
Professional door-to-door salesman, and boy do I
just want a moment, just one moment of your time-
precious time I sure do understand- but a moment
none-the-less, to talk to you slash to talk WITH you
about a fantastic deal, you see I've got something in
this briefcase I really want to show you—

MAX: —I don't think so.
Please go away—

ARTHUR: (*Pushing his way in*) now wait wait wait just a
minute miss— (?)

MAX: Oh
Max

But
You /can't come in—

ARTHUR: /MAX! What a beautiful name for a beautiful
lady
has anyone ever told you that you smell like
evergreens and damp earth and dried blood and WOW
oh WOW what nice eyes you have—

MAX: —you have to go—

ARTHUR: —wait—

MAX: —I don't have time for this /right now—

ARTHUR: —/because of the owl in the shower?

MAX: How—

ARTHUR: —now personally I believe the old oak is
an upgrade to your rather rudimentary toilet slash
plumbing system but that's just me. You don't seem
too thrilled but Maxine wow am I glad you let me in/
because I've got to just GOT to tell you all about what's
in my suitcase.

MAX: /I didn't.
…
…
How do you know?

ARTHUR: *(Making himself comfortable in the little motel
room.)* Well you see there are certain things that a man
with my profession makes it his job to know and in
addition there are things I hear along the way
From
Well associates.
You might call them.
I'm a salesman Max.
A door-to-door salesman. Knowing things is my trade.
.
You know.
This reminds me of a story.

MAX: I don't have any money.
I don't have any money I'm almost out of PTO
And
I'm pretty sure I'm off the Aspen project
I HOPE
I'm.
I.

ARTHUR: You sound overwhelmed.

MAX: I certainly feel overwhelmed.

ARTHUR: Point me to the kettle?

MAX: *(Pointing)* behind you.

ARTHUR: Ah. Still a kettle. It had the sense to wait a day
or two before—

MAX: —before?
What?
A shrub?
A monkey?

ARTHUR: A snapping turtle.
Lookay. The spout's gone a bit beak-ish.
But not yet.
I can still make coffee.

MAX: Why are you here?
Did Lisa send you?

ARTHUR: Oh no not Lisa.

MAX: *(Half rising)* Bryan?

ARTHUR: *(Gently)* No.

MAX: .

ARTHUR: And regarding money well.
Let us not concern ourselves as I have no use for such
coinage.
Sugar? Cream?

MAX: Black. Please.

(ARTHUR *and* MAX *drink their coffee.*)

ARTHUR: Wonderful coffee Max!

MAX: Your very first cup, I assume.

ARTHUR: But like I said. This reminds me of a story.
Have you ever heard about the two wolves—

MAX: —it's after midnight—

ARTHUR: —early bird and all that—

MAX: —there's an oak tree in my bathroom?

ARTHUR: I really think it spruces the place up!
(*Awkward pause*)
That joke would have landed if your toilet had turned
into a conifer.
Ah well.

(MAX *says nothing.*)

ARTHUR: About the two wolves.

(MAX *says nothing.*)

ARTHUR: And now you say: what about the two
wolves?

MAX: …
What about the two wolves?

ARTHUR: Stop me if you've heard this one.
There was a young woman.
Living in a run down motel.
Her name is not important.
And one night this young woman said to herself: I
don't feel so good.
I've got a fight in me and it feels like two wolves really
tearing one another up.
One of those wolves, she's fear. She's fear and sorrow
and confusion and desperation.
And the other wolf. Well she's anger. And she's
hungry.

This wolf inside this woman, Max. This anger wolf.
She's HUNGRY.

(MAX's *phone begins to buzz again.*)

ARTHUR: You're hungry. Aren't you Max?

MAX: Bryan sent you.
Didn't he?

ARTHUR: I'm here because you've got some wolves in
you.
But you've been feeding the wrong one.
Now may I show you what's in my suitcase?

(ARTHUR *takes out his suitcase.*
Slowly he undoes the clasps.
It opens to reveal a beautiful fur coat.)

MAX: What is it?
(*She is drawn to it*)

ARTHUR: Well Max.
This?
This can be yours.
If you decide you're ready to feed the right wolf.

MAX: Can I just—

(MAX *tries to touch the coat but* ARTHUR *snaps the suitcase*
shut.)

ARTHUR: Now. I'm not going to lie to you.
I work on commission.

MAX: Oh.
I told you.
I don't have any money.
My husband—my soon to be ex-husband. We have a
joint account.
I can't—

ARTHUR: —now wait a minute.
Did I name a price?
Did I throw any dollar signs at you?

Did I ask you to open up your coffers?
No. I did not.

MAX: Then what—

ARTHUR: When it's time. You'll know.

MAX: How will I know?

ARTHUR: You'll know.
(Rising)
Now.
I take it you're intrigued?
Gotta leave 'em guessing.
Keep them coming back.
WOW.
That coffee really hit the spot.

MAX: Are you leaving?

ARTHUR: Duty calls.
Places to be etcetera.

MAX: But.
The coat?

ARTHUR: Ah.
She's beautiful. Isn't she?

MAX: I don't understand.
I feel drawn to it.

ARTHUR: *(Smiling)* Well. Perhaps you'd like to hang on
to it?

MAX: I can't. Like I said. I don't have any money—

ARTHUR: —you're not listening, Max.
It's not money I'm after—

MAX: —then what?

ARTHUR: Something you're hardly using anymore.
Something you're already giving away!
Something you're replacing. With something better.

MAX: But what?

ARTHUR: You've already made the deal!
Listen
I'll let you in on a little secret.
I don't like to sell my goods to just anyone, you know
what I mean?

MAX: No.

ARTHUR: I'm not your run-of-the-mill American
salesman, you see what I'm saying?

MAX: Um.

ARTHUR: You and I have met before.

MAX: We have?

ARTHUR: It doesn't surprise me that you've forgotten
but I won't lie and tell you it doesn't hurt my feelings.

MAX: You're testing my patience Mr not-your-run-of-
the-mill-American-salesman.

ARTHUR: —
Of course.
I do sometimes forget how time works. Having been
outside of it myself for quite some—
Well.

.

You're already feeding your wolves. Aren't you, Max?
Stop acting like you're surprised to see me when I'm
only here to deliver your goods.

.

Hang on to this.

(ARTHUR *hands* MAX *the briefcase)*

ARTHUR: I think you'll be very satisfied with your
purchase—

MAX: —but—

(ARTHUR *is exiting.*
MAX *follows him, holding the briefcase.)*

MAX: —wait—

ARTHUR: —best of luck on your journey.
I'll see you soon. I suppose.
Best of luck.

(ARTHUR *exits.*
MAX is left standing holding the briefcase.
Slowly, she returns to the couch. She opens the briefcase.
She removes the coat.
She throws it on.
She howls a little howl.)

scene v:
the garbage kings

(*MAX on the couch with the coat.*
She smells something. Her stomach growls once more.
She follows her nose, taking the coat with her.
MAX goes outside.
She can smell something wonderful…
She stares at the stars.
The WOLF PACK enters. They are dragging a deer.
The bloody carcass sits in the middle of the half circle they've
formed.
They are euphoric. They can't wait to feed MAX.)

MAX: Hey.

PAMPLEMOUSSE: Hey.
We caught a deer.

MAX: I can smell it.

PAMPLEMOUSSE: It's pretty great huh?

MAX: Yeah.
(*She exits. Approaches the carcass.*
Maybe she strokes its hind legs.
She definitely sniffs it)
.

I'm pretty hungry.
I'm
Ravenous
And.
This smells—
Anyway.
It's like I've got this hole in me.
And it hurts a lot.
And I keep trying to fill it up with different stuff.
But nothing is working.
So.
Can I eat some of this carcass?

PAMPLEMOUSSE: Of course.

MAX: *(She tries to get some deer but her human hands are pretty feeble.)*
I don't have any claws so—

(PAMPLEMOUSSE *tears off a chunk of deer and passes it to* MAX:*)*

PAMPLEMOUSSE: I like your coat.

MAX: Thank you. I was cold.
(She regards the meat. The blood drips.
She licks the blood away from her hands.
She begins to eat the deer)
Oh.
Oh this is so good.
This is the greatest thing I've ever eaten.

PAMPLEMOUSSE: After the moon, it's pretty much the best thing in the world.

(Silence for a while as MAX *eats.)*

PAMPLEMOUSSE: We have a band

MAX: Oh?

PAMPLEMOUSSE: We're called the Garbage Kings.

MAX: I like it.
(She is almost done eating.
She burps indelicately.
She licks the blood from her fingers)

PAMPLEMOUSSE: Do you want to hear our music?

MAX: *(Eagerly.*
Savagely)
Yes.

PAMPLEMOUSSE: Alright.
This song is called *Rumpus.*

(The WOLF PACK *assemble their instruments.*
JET *has a guitar, RIFFRAF on the drums.*
RIFFRAF *counts down.)*

RIFFRAF: "Let the wild rumpus start!"™

(The WOLF PACK *begins a complicated dance.*
JET *plays guitar. It's a real party and it seems a little*
Dangerous.
More
more
more music
more dancing
louder
and louder
and more
and more dangerous
PAMPLEMOUSSE *encourages* MAX *to join in*
JET *strums the guitar big.*
The WOLF PACK *is panting tongues out happy happy.*
PAMPLEMOUSSE *and* MAX *have a moment.)*

PAMPLEMOUSSE: I've seen you around before

MAX: You have?

PAMPLEMOUSSE: I'm surprised you don't remember. It
was with your friend. The loud one.

MAX: I'm sorry. I'm not that person anymore.

PAMPLEMOUSSE: You're no person at all.

MAX: Everyone keeps saying that.

PAMPLEMOUSSE: How does it make you feel to hear it?

MAX: (*Flustered*) I—
Have you always been wolves?

PAMPLEMOUSSE: In this life?
In this forest?
Yeah.
I really like your coat.

MAX: Thank you.
I have a feeling it was expensive.

PAMPLEMOUSSE: How much did it cost?

MAX: I think it cost me everything I had.
But he was right.
I wasn't using it anyway.

PAMPLEMOUSSE: You should know something about
wolves
We hate metaphors.

MAX: Good to know.
You hate:
Running shoes
Metaphors—

PAMPLEMOUSSE: —I love
the moon. Your coat and—

MAX: —and?

PAMPLEMOUSSE: I really
Like.
The way you smell like blood.

(*The music is dying down.*
The other wolves pack up their instruments and begin to

trickle out
Off on another run.)

PAMPLEMOUSSE: We're gonna run again.

MAX: You run every night.

PAMPLEMOUSSE: Come with us.

MAX: *(She looks back at the motel room.)*
I should stay.

PAMPLEMOUSSE: What's so great about this place?

MAX: .
nothing. I guess.
I feel safe here.

PAMPLEMOUSSE: You hate it?
Great.
Let's leave.

(PAMPLEMOUSSE *pulls* MAX *away.)*

MAX: Wait—

PAMPLEMOUSSE: —they're gonna run without us—

(A distant howl.
PAMPLEMOUSSE *looks panicked. Maybe she returns the*
howl.)

MAX: Something weird is happening.

PAMPLEMOUSSE: What do you mean?

MAX: The forest.
It's
It's in there.
In my motel room.

PAMPLEMOUSSE: What
In that
Smelly human box?

MAX: I've got an owl in my shower.
.

I can feel my headache coming back.

PAMPLEMOUSSE: Show me.

(MAX *nods.*)

(MAX *and* PAMPLEMOUSSE *enter the motel room.*
Inside room #8 is louder than the forest.
Birds, crickets, peepers, and other creatures of the night are
in full swing.
The walls of the room are almost obscured with vines. The
old oak in the bathroom has spread to offer its cover to the
bed.
Somewhere a bullfrog utters a long low croak. There's a
pause and then a splash.)

MAX: I think there's a pond somewhere in here.

PAMPLEMOUSSE: If this is what the humans keep inside
then why don't they just live in the woods like us?

MAX: This isn't normal.

PAMPLEMOUSSE: I still don't understand.
Why do you like it so much?

MAX: It's quiet.

PAMPLEMOUSSE: Don't you feel safe with our pack?

MAX: No.
I don't feel safe anywhere.
.

I'm tired.
I don't think I want to run.

PAMPLEMOUSSE: *(Disappointed)* Okay.

MAX: I'm so full.
Thank you for the deer.
I needed that.

PAMPLEMOUSSE: It was our pleasure.
Pack takes care of pack.
You're a part of our pack.
I wish you would just howl with us.

MAX: Soon.
I can feel it.
Like.
I feel like it's going to be soon.
That I'll want to howl.

PAMPLEMOUSSE: Good.
(Fibbing a little)
Because Jet's getting impatient.

MAX: *(Understanding)* You like this coat?

PAMPLEMOUSSE: Yes.
You're starting to look like a wolf. That's a real
improvement.

MAX: Thank you.

PAMPLEMOUSSE: *(She approaches* MAX *but gently.)*
You still smell like fear.
Why is that?

MAX: I told you—

PAMPLEMOUSSE: What else?

(A moment.
PAMPLEMOUSSE *waits.*
MAX *decides.)*

MAX: Bryan.

PAMPLEMOUSSE: Bryan?

MAX: My husband he—
—I
(She freezes again.)

PAMPLEMOUSSE: *(A long low growl)* We'll kill him.

MAX: He'll kill you.

PAMPLEMOUSSE: No way.
We're the strongest.
And the smartest.
And we'll kill him.
And then you'll join our pack.
Because you'll feel safe.
Okay?

MAX: You can't—

PAMPLEMOUSSE: —because—

MAX: Because I thought I knew.
I thought I had it all figured out.
I got married.
I thought
I'm a part of my own little pack.
I know how to think like people.
I know how to move in a unit. A family unit.
Two for now and maybe, someday I don't know.
Maybe more?
Two people trying to be together trying to be tender
and kind to one another but
But that fell apart. He ruined that.
That fell apart and. I couldn't do anything to save it.
when it was. Now that it.
So.
I'm worried to give myself to another pack.
I need to learn. How to do things on my own.
Everywhere I go.
I've always needed help.
I'm small. And I'm quiet. My stomach is too soft and I
never have the right words.
You're asking me to howl and to run *with* you but
I'm worried that all I know how to do
is run away

PAMPLEMOUSSE: Then we'll teach you.
You've got good legs, strong teeth.

You got hungry when you smelled that blood.
The forest never scared you. Not once.
You know how to run. Away or towards? Doesn't
matter.
What matters?
Run with.
You run with me.
You run with us.
We will make you a wolf.
And you will be good.

MAX: .

.

.

(She hugs the coat around herself)
I don't think I'm brave enough.

PAMPLEMOUSSE: Maybe not by yourself.

(PAMPLEMOUSSE *leads* MAX *to a small patch of grass under
the oak branches.)*

PAMPLEMOUSSE: You're tired.
You said so.
Would you like to rest with me?

MAX. *(She nods, allows herself to be led.)* This coat feels
like it's a part of me.

PAMPLEMOUSSE: You wear it well.

(MAX *and* PAMPLEMOUSSE *curl up under the oak.)*

MAX: Pamplemousse?

PAMPLEMOUSSE: Yes?

MAX: I've never really been anything other than a
person.

.

What's it like being a wolf?

PAMPLEMOUSSE: Well it's the best thing in the world.

MAX: Even better than the moon?

PAMPLEMOUSSE: Without any doubt.

MAX: Even better than the deer?

PAMPLEMOUSSE: With great certainty.

MAX: And I'll really be brave?

PAMPLEMOUSSE: We'll all be brave together.

(*A beat*)

MAX: And we can destroy him?

PAMPLEMOUSSE: If that's what you want.

MAX: Blood for blood?

PAMPLEMOUSSE: Blood for blood.

MAX: (*Sleepily*) Pack takes care of pack.

PAMPLEMOUSSE: Yes.

(MAX *is falling asleep.*
PAMPLEMOUSSE *watches her.*)

MAX: There should be a place, where only the things you want to happen, happen.

PAMPLEMOUSSE: I think you'll like the forest, Max.

MAX: What if (*Yawn*) it doesn't like me?

(*All around* MAX *and* PAMPLEMOUSSE, *the forest blooms.*)

PAMPLEMOUSSE: I don't think you should worry about that.

MAX: Don't let go of my hand okay? Even after I fall asleep?

PAMPLEMOUSSE: I won't.

MAX: Will you tell me about the way things will be? So I can fall asleep and dream about it?

PAMPLEMOUSSE: .
There will be laughter.
And feasting.
And we will run.

And we will sing.
And maybe someday we will find a small boat.
Because here there are trees
but beyond the trees a cove
and an ocean on the other side of that.
You and I will charter a ship.
And it will never capsize.
And we'll take all of our friends.
And you will never be hungry
And you will never be lonely
And we will find forest after forest
Everywhere
And run
Until we grow old.
.

Was that okay?
Was that a good story?

(MAX *is sleeping.*
PAMPLEMOUSSE *rests her head on* MAX's *shoulder.*)

scene vi:
more casserole

(The next morning
Light trickles into the room.
MAX *is curled up under the coat. She stretches and begins to*
wake up.
PAMPLEMOUSSE *is gone.*
MAX *looks around. Confused*
A knock on the door)

LISA: Hello?

MAX: Oh.
Oh!
One minute.

(MAX *removes the coat.*
Looks for somewhere to stash it.
Drapes it on a branch for now.
There's no hiding the forest in her motel room though.
With some resignation, she answers the door.)

LISA: Here.

(LISA *passes* MAX *a casserole and strides into the room.*
Plants herself on a couch. She doesn't see to notice the forest
surrounding them.)

LISA: put that in the fridge.

MAX: Can you see the forest?

LISA: What forest? The one outdoors that we're about
to bulldoze? Yes, and it continues to be an eyesore.

MAX: No, the—
Nevermind.

LISA: Put that in the fridge.

MAX: It won't fit.

LISA: Ask me how the meeting went?

MAX: What—

LISA: —Aspen Grove. The condos. Ask me.

MAX: How—

LISA: —terrible. They're backing out.

MAX: What do you mean?

LISA: They're getting cold feet. Someone else wants to
acquire the land.

MAX: Who?

LISA: The government.

MAX: This land?
This motel?

LISA: They have the same idea we do minus the condos.

.

I needed you.

MAX: I'm sorry.
Maybe it will fall through.

LISA: It doesn't matter.
If not here than somewhere else.
Aspen is happening.

MAX: I'm sure.

LISA: They're going to lay you off.

MAX: *(Kind of interested)*
Oh?

LISA: We can't wait for you forever.

MAX: I know.

LISA: When are you coming back?

MAX: I don't know.

LISA: *(Losing it a little)*
You don't know anything!
(Finding her center)
I'm sorry.
I'm a little high strung.
I'm upset.
I'm upset about Aspen.
It's fine.

.

.

.

I saw Bryan today.

MAX: Oh.

LISA: Oh don't "oh" me Maxine. He misses you.

MAX: I don't care.

LISA: You're just worked up right now.

MAX: I am not worked up.
I'm
(*She searches.*)
I'm—
I never want to see him again.
He terrifies me.
He's unpredictable.
I don't know what he'll do.

LISA: Oh enough with the dramatics.
He's sorry. He told me so himself.
He just wants you back.
.
The next time he calls, just answer the phone.
Okay?

MAX: No.

LISA: Oh fine Maxine but you're doing this to yourself.
He's going to come looking for you
You haven't signed the papers yet.
You know there's a reason.
You're hesitating for a reason.

MAX: I just—
I need more time.

LISA: I think the two of you just need to sit down face
to face and find time to talk to one another. Really
work this out.

MAX: Don't tell him where I am

LISA: Oh.

MAX: You told him.

LISA: (*Looking out the window*)
Oh
Max
The wolves.

MAX: Did. You. Tell. Him. Where. I. Am?

LISA: Okay don't freak out. But the wolves are at your door—

MAX: Lisa answer me—

LISA: —but I'm here for you. You call animal control. I'll scare them off okay?

MAX: What?

(LISA *searches in her purse for the air horn.*
She holds it triumphantly over her head.
She swings the door open.
She regards the WOLF PACK.
She blasts the horn.
MAX *covers her ears.*
The WOLF PACK *doesn't move.*)

LISA: Stubborn mother effers huh?

(*She bends down and scoops up a handful of rocks*
she begins to throw the rocks at the WOLF PACK.
JET *and* RIFFRAF *bristle.*
CRACKER JACK *begins to advance.*)

MAX: WHAT ARE YOU DOING?

LISA: You just wait and see.
WE ARE PEOPLE!
YOU ARE DIRTY FOREST ANIMALS!
GET OUT OF HERE.

(LISA *throws more rocks.*
The WOLF PACK *still advancing*)

MAX: STOP!

(MAX *runs in front of* LISA
slams the door shut
a rock hits her.)

LISA: Oh my god.
Max.
I'm so sorry.

MAX: Get out.

LISA: What do you mean?

MAX: You can't stay here.
We're not friends anymore.

LISA: You've gone totally savage.
We are BEST friends Maxine you said so yourself.
.
I took you to my oracle.

MAX: I hate you.

LISA: MAX.

MAX: I hate you get out.

LISA: Well I cannot leave that way.
The wolves are out there.

(LISA and MAX *stare at one another for a minute.*
MAX *breaks the spell. She opens the door.*
She speaks to the WOLF PACK.
To the WOLF PACK, *her language makes sense.*
But to LISA *it sounds like a series of growls and whines.*)

MAX: Hey. I'm going to get rid of her. Okay?
But you have to leave.

LISA: What are you saying to them?
Are you speaking their language?
Do they have LANGUAGE?

MAX: You have to go.

RIFFRAF: No way.
We're gonna eat her.
She can't throw rocks at us

AJAX: YA SOMEONE TELL THAT BITCH SHE
FUCKED UP

PAMPLEMOUSSE: We're gonna eat out her heart—

MAX: You can't have her heart okay you just can't

AJAX: WHY NOT?
SHE MADE ME BLEED
BLOOD FOR BLOOD

MAX: If you guys fuck up.
They'll round you up and kill you.

PAMPLEMOUSSE: Why do you care?
You're not part of our pack.

MAX: I care. Okay I just.
I still need more time

PAMPLEMOUSSE: We need to move soon.
We can't stay here much longer.
We're almost out of deer.

MAX: Just a little longer please.

PAMPLEMOUSSE: …
We won't eat her heart today.
She can leave.

(Growls of protest)

PAMPLEMOUSSE: But

you need to howl with us soon.

Or we're going to leave you.

You're not human anymore Max.

You can't go back.

You need a pack.

Join our pack.

MAX: .
.
.

Thankyoufornoteatingmyfriendsheart.
(She slams the door shut)

LISA: *(Shaken)*
What. Was that?

MAX: I convinced them not to eat your heart.
You did a terrible thing.
You can't treat my friends like that

LISA: Your friends?
Oh Max.
And what was that
You were doing
You were growling?
And
Whining?
Like a wolf.

MAX: I don't know I talk to them and they talk back.
(She looks out the window)
Okay. They're gone. You can leave now

(LISA *hesitates like she wants to help* MAX.
But then she gathers her things.)

LISA: You've changed.
Listen. Bryan knows you're here.
.

He *cares* about you okay?
He wants to help you
And you haven't signed the paperwork.
So just. Listen to him okay?
He's a *good* man.

MAX: *(Softly)* he raped me.

LISA: *(She takes a moment.*
She decides she didn't hear that.)
Max—
.

He's a good man.
(She exits.)

(A silence
Darkness)

scene vii:

(MAX alone in the dark.
She curls up on the grass.)

(Time passes.)

(Howling
Whining
Pawing at the door)

(MAX does not respond.)

MAX: GO AWAY.

(MAX's phone buzzes.
This goes on a while.)

MAX: SHUT UP!

(Silence. Just the forest and all of its sounds
Almost all the furniture is gone now.
The coffee pot has indeed been replaced by a snapping turtle.)

(The sounds of running water
Peepers
Cicadas
The forest as it exists at night.)

(The WOLF PACK howls.)

(MAX is trying to sleep but just tossing and turning.)

(In the distance, a large vehicle approaches. Beams of lights
from headlights sweep room 8.)

(MAX sits up.)

(The truck slows to a stop.)

(Footsteps)

(A knock)

MAX: No.

(BRYAN *is at the door.*)

BRYAN: Max?

.

Max it's me.

.

C'mon Maxine this has gone on long enough.

.

.

.

Answer the door. I just want to talk.

.

.

Answer the goddamn door Max.

.

.

Sorry. I lost my temper. For a second. It won't happen
again.

.

I haven't gotten the paper work yet.
I assume
I assume that means.

.

Lisa thinks we should just talk.
She's really worried about you.
I'm really worried about you.
We all just want what's best for YOU, Maxine.

.

I'm sorry about Aspen Grove.
I know you were really passionate about that but.
Lisa says you'll find another lot. So.
I think there's time.
You can go back to work. Tell them you needed some
time to think.
It's not too late.

.

.

.

I want you back Max.

.

I'm sorry I.
I was confused. I thought you.
It just. We hadn't.
You hadn't touched me in so long. I thought maybe.
Maybe I could remind you

.

.

Max?

.

.

.

MAX.

.

.

.

Goddamnit Max I will break down this door.

(MAX *stands.*)

MAX: please go away.

(BRYAN *presses himself to the door. He seems vulnerable in his need to talk to* MAX.)

BRYAN: Max?
Is that you?
Let me in please.

MAX: Go.
Away.

BRYAN: Honey I just want to talk.

MAX: I don't ever want to see you again.

BRYAN: Sweetheart. That's not true.
If that was true you would have signed those papers.
We're still married.

We're still husband and wife.
You need to come home.

MAX: No.
I live here now.

BRYAN: What here?
In room #8 of Shady Pines?

MAX: Yes.
The coffee is terrible.
The forest is loud.
I love it.

BRYAN: Let me in.

MAX: I can't.

BRYAN: We need to talk.

MAX: *(A deep breath)* You need to leave.

BRYAN: GODDAMNIT MAX
(He slams himself against the door.)

*(*MAX *is in a panic. She freezes.*
BRYAN *continues to throw himself against the door.*
MAX *takes a deep breath.*
MAX *begins to howl.*
BRYAN *continues to charge the door.*
In the distance,* MAX'*s howling is returned.*
BRYAN *slams into the door.*
The door gives in.)*

*(*BRYAN *stumbles into the room.*
He steadies himself.
He and* MAX *stare at one another.)*

MAX: Bryan—

BRYAN: —now. Finally.
We have a chance to talk—

(In the distance, the sound of the WOLF PACK *howling
grows closer*

and closer.
Until…
The WOLF PACK *enters.*
JET strums the guitar big.
The WOLF PACK *is spooky.*
Vicious
They circle the motel room which is now the forest clearing
which is now silent but for the growling of the WOLF
PACK.)

MAX: I said.
LEAVE.

BRYAN: *(Regarding the* WOLF PACK*)* what is this
(Regarding the room) what's happening in here?
Max.
You're wild.
You're a wild thing now.
Why won't you just—
(He holds out a hand.)
Come with me.

(A tension that builds as MAX *finds strength:)*

MAX: Maybe.
Maybe I'm wild.
I haven't really felt like myself. Lately.
Lately, I've been spending a lot of time running with
the wrong crowd.

BRYAN: What the hell is going on—

MAX: —you don't know me anymore.

(The WOLF PACK *is advancing.)*

MAX: I hardly know myself.

(The WOLF PACK *is licking their lips.)*

MAX: But I know one thing.

BRYAN: Max—

MAX: I don't belong to you.

PAMPLEMOUSSE: You howled.
That means you've decided.
Have you decided?

MAX: Yes.

PAMPLEMOUSSE: This guy giving you trouble?

MAX: Yes.

PAMPLEMOUSSE: Need a hand?

MAX: That would be nice.
.
I may be a Wild Thing now…
.

.

.
So I guess.
WE'LL EAT YOU UP!

(JET *plays the guitar as the* WOLF PACK *descends on* BRYAN.)

(BRYAN *doesn't stand a chance. By the end of the refrain, he's gone.*)

(*Eaten up*)

(*Wolf bait*)

(*Yum*)

(MAX *and the* WOLF PACK *stare down at what is left of* BRYAN.)

MAX: My body doesn't belong to you.
And it doesn't belong to the wolves.
I belong to myself.
I will make my own choices.

(*The* WOLF PACK *brings* MAX *the fur coat. They hold it open and she puts it on.*
PAMPLEMOUSSE *approaches with a wolf mask. She places this on* MAX.)

MAX: I choose. I choose wolf. I'm a wolf now.
.

PAMPLEMOUSSE: Welcome to the pack. You're a king now Max. You're a garbage king.
Here's your crown.

MAX: Thank you.
I don't know how to play any instruments.

PAMPLEMOUSSE: That's okay. We can teach you.

MAX: Is he dead?
Is he really dead?

(The WOLF PACK *nods.)*

MAX: .
I guess it doesn't matter if I sign the papers then.
.

What happens now?

PAMPLEMOUSSE: *(Looking back at the motel which is now completely taken over by the forest.)*
No more human house.

MAX: No.
I told Lisa I hate her.
She's against me.
Now we're enemies.
.

.

I don't think I know how to talk to people anymore.

(A long silence.
The wind blows through the old oak.
JET *starts a howl.*
The rest of the pack picks it up.
MAX *and the* WOLF PACK *howl for a long time.*
.

Silence.
And then.

MAX: Let's run.

(Drums
The forest
Darkness)

END OF PLAY

* 9 7 9 8 8 8 8 5 6 0 2 5 9 *